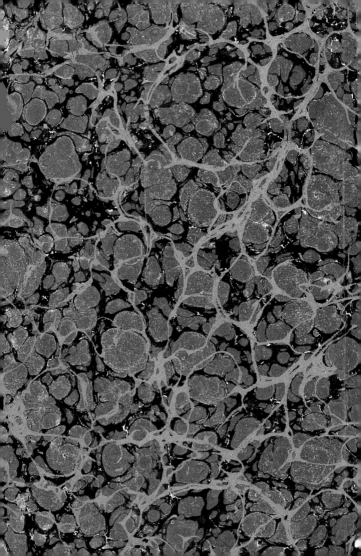

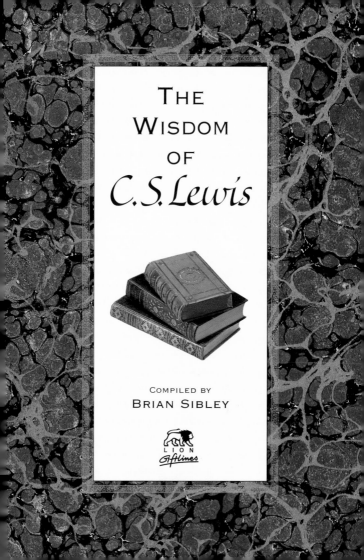

THE
WISDOM
OF
C.S. Lewis

COMPILED BY
BRIAN SIBLEY

LION
Giftlines

This edition copyright © 1997 Lion Publishing

Published by
Lion Publishing plc
Sandy Lane West, Oxford, England
ISBN 0 7459 3932 5

First edition 1997
10 9 8 7 6 5 4 3 2 1 0

A catalogue record for this book is available
from the British Library

Printed and bound in Singapore

Series editor: Meryl Doney
Project editor: Angela Handley
Jacket designer: Jonathan Roberts
Cover and first page illustration: David Axtell

Contents

INTRODUCTION 6

THE GREAT CREATOR 11

DARK POWERS 17

THE STILL POINT OF HISTORY 23

CHOICES 29

THE LIFE OF FAITH 35

WORLDS BEYOND 41

'C.S. Lewis gave God back to the people.' That is how I summed up Lewis' career when, a few years ago, *The Sunday Times* listed him among 'The 1,000 Makers of the Twentieth Century'. An extravagant claim, some might think, but it is a fact that no spiritual writer of our age has made a greater impact on humanity or left a more enduring heritage.

C.S. Lewis – or, as he was always known to family and friends, 'Jack' – was born on the 29 November 1898, on the outskirts of Belfast, Northern Ireland. His mother was a clergyman's daughter and he was raised in a nominally Christian environment, although religion was more of a duty than a joy and failed to evoke in him the excitement and wonder which he experienced when his Irish nurse told him tales of leprechauns, heroes and the pagan gods of old Ireland. Those stories began Jack's life-long love of legend and mythology which later – baptised, as it were, by his Christian faith – was a recurrent inspiration for his own storytelling.

When Jack Lewis was ten years old, his mother developed cancer. The young boy dredged his shallow faith for help: prayed first for her recovery and then, when she died, for a miracle to bring her back to life. The seeming denial of these requests, pushed him towards a rejection of God; but, deep inside him, something was still seeking an answer, reaching out for understanding. Many years later – long after he had written books which tackled the subjects of pain, death and miracles – he would stand beside the bed of another woman whom he loved and re-live the anger, fear and doubts that he had experienced as a child.

Throughout his school and university days, and his time serving in the armed forces during the First World War, Jack found himself being alternately drawn to Christianity and repelled by it. He would eventually describe these years as ones in which the Great Angler was fishing for his soul. He was thirty years old when God eventually 'hooked' him and reeled in the line.

A Fellow of Magdalen College, Oxford, Jack Lewis came under the influence of several academic friends – among them J.R.R. Tolkien, the author of *The Lord of the Rings* – who shared his passion for legend and story, but who also happened to have a Christian faith. On a night in 1929, Jack 'gave in, and admitted that God was God, and knelt and prayed'. He was, he later said, 'the most dejected and reluctant convert in all England'. Even so, the struggle was just beginning and it was another two years before Jack was prepared to accept that Jesus was the Son of God. Perhaps it was only because of his own difficulties in coming to a faith in Christ, that he clearly understood the disbelief of others and attempted to address their doubts and objections with honesty and frankness.

His first book of apologetics, *The Pilgrim's Regress*, was published in 1933 – just two years after his full conversion to

Christianity. Other books followed including *The Problem of Pain* and *The Screwtape Letters*, a cunning inversion of the Christian epistle in which a senior devil offers advice to a young demon on how to prevent a human subject from becoming – and then remaining – a Christian.

In 1941, the BBC invited Jack to give a series of radio talks about Christian belief. 'I think they asked me,' he said, 'because I am a layman, not a clergyman; and because I had been a non-Christian for many years.' Those talks – delivered with a clarity and directness that is still sharp and penetrating fifty years later – were published first as a series of pamphlets and then, edited and expanded into book form, as *Mere Christianity*.

Jack Lewis had an extraordinary – and undoubtedly God-given – ability for discerning, and confronting, the difficult questions which human beings habitually raise on matters of faith and belief. More than that, he possessed the wisdom and daring to offer answers in a compelling and authoritative voice. He spoke and wrote with spiritual conviction and all the precision of a dedicated word-smith; as one of the characters in his novel, *Till We have Faces*, remarks: 'To say the very thing you really mean, the whole of it, nothing more or less or other than what you really mean; that is the whole art and joy of words.'

That art and joy can be seen in such Christian writings as *The Great Divorce*, *Miracles*, *Reflections on the Psalms*, *The Four Loves* and *Prayer: Letters to Malcolm*, as well as in numerous talks, sermons and essays published since his death in 1963. His writings, however, ranged widely – poetry, novels, science-fiction and children's stories – and they were all, in time, touched or transfused by his Christian faith.

The publication, in 1950, of *The Lion, the Witch and the Wardrobe*, the first of the seven 'Chronicles of Narnia', established Jack Lewis as one of the most original children's writers of his day. The durability of these books across several generations, have secured them the status of classics. More significantly, their allegorical depiction of the death and resurrection of Jesus and aspects of the Christian life have opened the eyes of many young readers to the spiritual dimensions of the world around them.

In recent years, through books, plays and films about Jack Lewis' life – and, in particular, about his relationship with the American writer Joy Davidman who died of cancer shortly after their marriage – the teller of tales, the weaver of fantasies has himself been turned into a mythic figure; a late twentieth-century icon for pain and suffering.

It is true that Jack's anguish at the loss of a love so lately won brutally confronted him with deep, dark doubts and he painfully chronicled his emotions in *A Grief Observed*. But although, in bereavement, he revisited old sorrows and despairs, perhaps even questioned the confident arguments in his very own books, he emerged from this bitterly painful experience, as he did from every experience in his life, a humbler, wiser man and a more devout, confident and compassionate Christian.

With hindsight, it is possible to see Jack Lewis' whole life as undergoing a constant process of transformation through the power of God's invading love. That he struggled so long and hard against that invasion makes him our brother in adversity; that he eventually – and repeatedly – submitted to it, accepted it with joy, and witnessed to it in his daily life, surely makes him our teacher.

BRIAN SIBLEY

The Great Creator

GOD WHISPERS
TO US IN OUR
PLEASURES, SPEAKS
TO US IN OUR
CONSCIENCE,
BUT SHOUTS IN OUR
PAINS: IT IS HIS
MEGAPHONE TO ROUSE
A DEAF WORLD.

FROM
THE PROBLEM OF PAIN

THE GIFT OF LOVE

We begin at the real beginning, with love as the Divine energy. This primal love is Gift-love. In God there is no hunger that needs to be filled, only plenteousness that desires to give.

FROM *THE FOUR LOVES*

THE ARCHANGEL AND THE WORM

The relation between Creator and creature is, of course, unique, and cannot be paralleled by any relations between one creature and another. God is both further from us, and nearer to us, than any other being. He is further from us because the sheer difference between that which has Its principle of being in Itself and that to which being is communicated, is one compared with which the difference between an archangel and a worm is quite insignificant. He makes, we are made: he is original, we derivative. But at the same time, and for the same reason, the intimacy between God and even the meanest creature is closer than any that creatures can attain with one another. Our life is, at every moment, supplied by him: our tiny, miraculous power of free will only operates on bodies which his continual energy keeps in existence – our very power to think is his power communicated to us.

FROM *THE PROBLEM OF PAIN*

TO BORROW SIXPENCE

I think every one who has some vague belief in God, until he becomes a Christian, has the idea of an exam or of a bargain in his mind. The first result of real Christianity is to blow that idea into bits… God has been waiting for the moment at which you discover that there is no question of earning a pass mark in this exam or putting him in your debt.

Then comes another discovery. Every faculty you have, your power of thinking or of moving your limbs from moment to moment, is given you by God. If you devoted every moment of your whole life exclusively to his service you could not give him anything that was not in a sense his own already. So that when we talk of a man doing anything for God or giving anything to God, I will tell you what it is really like. It is like a small child going to its father and saying, 'Daddy, give me sixpence to buy you a birthday present.' Of course, the father does, and he is pleased with the child's present. It is all very nice and proper, but only an idiot would think that the father is sixpence to the good on the transaction. When a man has made these two discoveries God can really get to work. It is after this that real life begins.

FROM *MERE CHRISTIANITY*

DIVINE JUSTICE

God in his mercy made
The fixed pains of Hell.
That misery might be stayed,
God in his mercy made
Eternal bounds and bade
Its waves no further swell.
God in his mercy made
The fixed pains of Hell.

FROM *POEMS*

THE KEY TO THE LOCK

Be sure that the ins and outs of your individuality are no mystery to him; and one day they will no longer be a mystery to you. The mould in which a key is made would be a strange thing, if you had never seen a key: and the key itself a strange thing if you had never seen a lock. Your soul has a curious shape because it is a hollow made to fit a particular swelling in the infinite contours of the divine substance, or a key to unlock one of the doors in the house with many mansions.

FROM *THE PROBLEM OF PAIN*

Dark Powers

THE SAFEST ROAD
TO HELL IS THE
GRADUAL ONE —
THE GENTLE SLOPE,
SOFT UNDERFOOT,
WITHOUT SUDDEN
TURNINGS, WITHOUT
MILESTONES,
WITHOUT
SIGNPOSTS.

FROM
THE SCREWTAPE LETTERS

THE DARK POWER

Wwhat is the problem? A universe that contains much that is obviously bad and apparently meaningless, but containing creatures like ourselves who know that it is bad and meaningless. There are only two views that face all the facts. One is the Christian view that this is a good world that has gone wrong, but still retains the memory of what it ought to have been. The other is the view called Dualism. Dualism means the belief that there are two equal and independent powers at the back of everything, one of them good and the other bad, and that this universe is the battlefield in which they fight out an endless war…

One of the things that surprised me when I first read the New Testament seriously was that it talked so much about a Dark Power in the universe – a mighty evil spirit who was held to be the Power behind death and disease, and sin. The difference is that Christianity thinks this Dark Power was created by God, and was good when he was created, and went wrong. Christianity agrees with Dualism that this universe is at war. But it does not think this is a war between independent powers. It thinks it is a civil war, a rebellion, and that we are living in a part of the universe occupied by the rebel.

FROM *MERE CHRISTIANITY*

TALK OF THE DEVIL

Enemy-occupied territory – that is what this world is. Christianity is the story of how the rightful king has landed, you might say landed in disguise, and is calling us all to take part in a great campaign of sabotage. When you go to church you are really listening-in to the secret wireless from our friends: that is why the enemy is so anxious to prevent us from going. He does it by playing on our conceit and laziness and intellectual snobbery. I know someone will ask me, 'Do you really mean, at this time of day, to re-introduce our old friend the devil – hoofs and horns and all?' Well, what the time of day has to do with it I do not know… But in other respects my answer is 'Yes, I do.' I do not claim to know anything about his personal appearance. If anybody really wants to know him better I would say to that person, 'Don't worry. If you really want to, you will. Whether you'll like it when you do is another question.'

FROM *MERE CHRISTIANITY*

FALLEN ANGEL

To be bad, [the devil] must exist and have intelligence and will. But existence, intelligence and will are in themselves good. Therefore he must be getting them from the Good Power: even to be bad he must borrow or steal from his opponent. And do you now begin to see why Christianity has always said that the devil is a fallen angel? That is not a mere story for the children. It is a real recognition of the fact that evil is a parasite, not an original thing. The powers which enable evil to carry on are powers given it by goodness. All the things which enable a bad man to be effectively bad are in themselves good things – resolution, cleverness, good looks, existence itself.

FROM *MERE CHRISTIANITY*

To Be Like Gods

How did the Dark Power go wrong? Here, no doubt, we ask a question to which human beings cannot give an answer with any certainty. A reasonable (and traditional) guess, based on our own experiences of going wrong, can, however, be offered. The moment you have a self at all, there is a possibility of putting yourself first – wanting to be the centre – wanting to be God, in fact. That was the sin of Satan: and that was the sin he taught the human race… What Satan put into the heads of our remote ancestors was the idea that they could 'be like gods' – could set up on their own as if they had created themselves – be their own masters – invent some sort of happiness for themselves outside God, apart from God. And out of that hopeless attempt has come nearly all that we call human history – money, poverty, ambition, war, prostitution, classes, empires, slavery – the long terrible story of man trying to find something other than God which will make him happy.

FROM *MERE CHRISTIANITY*

A WORD FROM SCREWTAPE

'To secure the damnation of these little souls, these creatures that have almost ceased to be individual, is a laborious and tricky work. But if proper pains and skill are expended, you can be fairly confident of the result. The great sinners *seem* easier to catch. But then they are incalculable. After you have played them for seventy years, the Enemy may snatch them from your claws in the seventy-first. They are capable, you see, of real repentance. They are conscious of real guilt. They are, if things take the wrong turn, as ready to defy the social pressures around them for the Enemy's sake as they were to defy them for ours. It is in some ways more troublesome to track and swat an evasive wasp than to shoot, at close range, a wild elephant. But the elephant is more troublesome if you miss.'

FROM *SCREWTAPE PROPOSES A TOAST*

The Still Point of History

A MAN WHO WAS
MERELY A MAN AND SAID
THE SORT OF THINGS
JESUS SAID WOULD NOT
BE A GREAT MORAL
TEACHER. HE WOULD
EITHER BE A LUNATIC —
ON A LEVEL WITH THE
MAN WHO SAYS HE IS A
POACHED EGG — OR ELSE
HE WOULD BE THE
DEVIL OF HELL. YOU
MUST MAKE YOUR
CHOICE.

FROM *MERE CHRISTIANITY*

THE SHOCKING PARADOX

There was a man born among these Jews who claimed to be, or to be the son of, or to be 'one with', the Something which is at once the awful haunter of nature and the giver of the moral law. The claim is so shocking – a paradox, and even a horror, which we may easily be lulled into taking too lightly – that only two views of this man are possible. Either he was a raving lunatic of an unusually abominable type, or else he was, and is, precisely what he said. There is no middle way. If the records make the first hypothesis unacceptable, you must submit to the second. And if you do that, all else that is claimed by Christians becomes credible – that this Man, having been killed, was yet alive, and that his death, in some manner incomprehensible to human thought, has effected a real change in our relations to the 'awful' and 'righteous' Lord, and a change in our favour.

FROM *THE PROBLEM OF PAIN*

THE STARTLING CLAIM

He claims to forgive sins. He says he has always existed. He says he is coming to judge the world at the end of time… Now unless the speaker is God, this is really so preposterous as to be comic. We can all understand how a man forgives offences against himself. You tread on my toe and I forgive you, you steal my money and I forgive you. But what should we make of a man, himself unrobbed and untrodden on, who announced that he forgave you for treading on other men's toes and stealing other men's money? Asinine fatuity is the kindest description we should give of his conduct. Yet this is what Jesus did. He told people that their sins were forgiven, and never waited to consult all the other people whom their sins had undoubtedly injured. He unhesitatingly behaved as if he was the party chiefly concerned, the person chiefly offended in all offences. This makes sense only if he really was the God whose laws are broken and whose love is wounded in every sin.

FROM *MERE CHRISTIANITY*

FOOTING THE BILL

The one [theory about Christ's death] most people have heard is the one... about our being let off because Christ had volunteered to bear a punishment instead of us. Now on the face of it that is a very silly theory. If God was prepared to let us off, why on earth did he not do so? And what possible point could there be in punishing an innocent person instead? None at all that I can see, if you are thinking of punishment in the police-court sense. On the other hand, if you think of a debt, there is plenty of point in a person who has some assets paying it on behalf of someone who has not. Or if you take 'paying the penalty', not in the sense of being punished, but in the more general sense of 'standing the racket or 'footing the bill', then, of course, it is a matter of common experience that, when one person has got himself into a hole, the trouble of getting him out usually falls on a kind friend.

FROM *MERE CHRISTIANITY*

LIKE LIGHTNING

We believe that the death of Christ is just that point in history at which something absolutely unimaginable from outside shows through into our own world. And if we cannot picture even the atoms of which our own world is built, of course we are not going to be able to picture this. Indeed, if we found that we could fully understand it, that very fact would show it was not what it professes to be – the inconceivable, the uncreated, the thing from beyond nature, striking down into nature like lightning. You may ask what good it will be to us if we do not understand it. But that is easily answered. A man can eat his dinner without understanding exactly how food nourishes him. A man can accept what Christ has done without knowing how it works: indeed, he certainly would not know how it works until he has accepted it.

FROM *MERE CHRISTIANITY*

THE ONLY CHOICE

You must make your choice. Either this man was, and is, the Son of God: or else a madman or something worse. You can shut him up for a fool, you can spit at him and kill him as a demon; or you can fall at his feet and call him Lord and God. But let us not come with any patronising nonsense about his being a great human teacher. He has not left that open to us. He did not intend to.

FROM *MERE CHRISTIANITY*

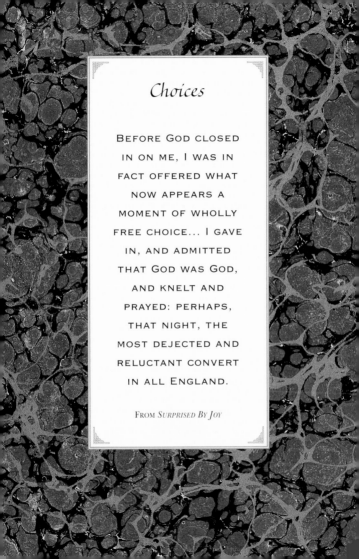

Choices

BEFORE GOD CLOSED
IN ON ME, I WAS IN
FACT OFFERED WHAT
NOW APPEARS A
MOMENT OF WHOLLY
FREE CHOICE... I GAVE
IN, AND ADMITTED
THAT GOD WAS GOD,
AND KNELT AND
PRAYED: PERHAPS,
THAT NIGHT, THE
MOST DEJECTED AND
RELUCTANT CONVERT
IN ALL ENGLAND.

FROM *SURPRISED BY JOY*

FUEL FOR THE SPIRIT

God made us: invented us as a man invents an engine. A car is made to run on petrol, and it would not run properly on anything else. Now God designed the human machine to run on himself. He himself is the fuel our spirits were designed to burn, or the food our spirits were designed to feed on. There is no other. That is why it is just no good asking God to make us happy in our own way without bothering about religion. God cannot give us a happiness and peace apart from himself, because it is not there. There is no such thing.

FROM *MERE CHRISTIANITY*

INFECTIOUS GOODNESS

Now the whole offer which Christianity makes is this: that we can, if we let God have his way, come to share in the life of Christ. If we do, we shall then be sharing a life which was begotten, not made, which always has existed and always will exist. Christ is the Son of God. If we share in this kind of life we also shall be sons of God. We shall love the Father as he does and the Holy Ghost will arise in us. He came to this world and became a man in order to spread to other men the kind of life he has – by what I call 'good infection'. Every Christian is to become a little Christ. The whole purpose of becoming a Christian is simply nothing else.

FROM *MERE CHRISTIANITY*

THE UNSAFE INVESTMENT

There is no safe investment. To love at all is to be vulnerable. Love anything, and your heart will certainly be wrung and possibly be broken. If you want to make sure of keeping it intact, you must give your heart to no one, not even to an animal. Wrap it carefully round with hobbies and little luxuries; avoid all entanglements; lock it up safe in the casket or coffin of your selfishness. But in that casket – safe, dark, motionless, airless – it will change. It will not be broken; it will become unbreakable, impenetrable, irredeemable. The alternative to tragedy, or at least to the risk of tragedy, is damnation. The only place outside Heaven where you can be perfectly safe from all the dangers and perturbations of love is Hell.

FROM *THE FOUR LOVES*

A LITTLE CLEAR PICTURE

'The choice of ways is before you. Neither is closed. Any man may choose eternal death. Those who choose it will have it. But if ye are trying to leap on into eternity, if ye are trying to seek the final state of all things as it *will* be (for so ye must speak) when there are no more possibilities left but only the Real, then ye ask what cannot be answered to mortal ears. Time is the very lens through which ye see – small and clear, as men see through the wrong end of a telescope – something that would otherwise be too big for ye to see at all. That thing is Freedom: the gift whereby ye most resemble your Maker and are yourselves parts of eternal reality. But ye can see it only through the lens of Time, in a little clear picture, through the inverted telescope. It is a picture of moments following one another and yourself in each moment making some choice that might have been otherwise.'

FROM *THE GREAT DIVORCE*

MERE MORALITY

All right, Christianity will do you good – a great deal more good than you ever wanted or expected. And the first bit of good it will do you is to hammer into your head (you won't enjoy *that*!) the fact that what you have hitherto called 'good' – all that about 'leading a decent life' and 'being kind' – isn't quite the magnificent and all-important affair you supposed. It will teach you that in fact you can't be 'good' (not for twenty-four hours) on your own moral efforts. And then it will teach you that even if you were, you still wouldn't have achieved the purpose for which you were created. Mere *morality* is not the end of life. You were made for something quite different from that.

FROM 'MAN OR RABBIT?'
IN *GOD IN THE DOCK*

The Life of Faith

A MAN CAN'T BE
ALWAYS DEFENDING
THE TRUTH; THERE
MUST BE A TIME TO
FEED ON IT.

FROM
*REFLECTIONS ON
THE PSALMS*

A PRAYER BEFORE PRAYING

The prayer preceding all prayers is, 'May it be the real I who speaks. May it be the real thou that I speak to.' Infinitely various are the levels from which we pray. Emotional intensity is in itself no proof of spiritual depth. If we pray in terror we shall pray earnestly; it only proves that terror is an earnest emotion. Only God himself can let the bucket down to the depths in us. And, on the other side, he must constantly work as the iconoclast. Every idea of him we form, he must in mercy shatter. The most blessed result of prayer would be to rise thinking, 'But I never knew before. I never dreamed…'

FROM *PRAYER: LETTERS TO MALCOLM*

TALKING IT OVER

Prayers are not always – in the crude, factual sense of the word – 'granted'. This is not because prayer is a weaker kind of causality, but because it is a stronger kind. When it 'works' at all it works unlimited by space and time. That is why God has retained a discretionary power of granting or refusing it; except on that condition prayer would destroy us. It is not unreasonable for a headmaster to say, 'Such and such things you may do according to the fixed rules of this school. But such and such other things are too dangerous to be left to general rules. If you want to do them you must come and make a request and talk over the whole matter with me in my study. And then – we'll see.'

FROM 'WORK AND PRAYER'
IN *UNDECEPTIONS*

INNUMERABLE CHOICES

People often think of Christian morality as a kind of bargain in which God says, 'If you keep a lot of rules I'll reward you, and if you don't I'll do the other thing.' I do not think that is the best way of looking at it. I would much rather say that every time you make a choice you are turning the central part of you, the part of you that chooses, into something a little different from what it was before. And taking your life as a whole, with all your innumerable choices, all your life long you are slowly turning this central thing either into a heavenly creature or into a hellish creature: either into a creature that is in harmony with God, and with other creatures, and with itself, or else into one that is in a state of war and hatred with God, and with its fellow-creatures, and with itself. To be the one kind of creature is heaven: that is, it is joy and peace and knowledge and power. To be the other means madness, horror, idiocy, rage, impotence, and eternal loneliness. Each of us at each moment is progressing to the one state or the other.

FROM *MERE CHRISTIANITY*

PRAYING AND DREAMING

Master, they say that when I seem
To be in speech with you,
Since you make no replies, it's all a dream
– One talker aping two.

They are half right, but not as they
Imagine; rather, I
Seek in myself the things I meant to say,
And lo! the wells are dry.

Then, seeing me empty, you forsake
The Listener's role, and through
My dead lips breathe and into
utterance wake
The thoughts I never knew.

And thus you neither need reply
Nor can; thus, while we seem
Two talking, thou art One forever, and I
No dreamer, but thy dream.

'PRAYER' FROM *POEMS*

THE INEXCUSABLE

To be a Christian means to forgive the inexcusable, because God has forgiven the inexcusable in you.

This is hard. It is perhaps not so hard to forgive a single great injury. But to forgive the incessant provocations of daily-life – to keep on forgiving the bossy mother-in-law, the bullying husband, the nagging wife, the selfish daughter, the deceitful son – how can we do it? Only, I think, by remembering where we stand, by meaning our words when we say in our prayers each night 'Forgive us our trespasses as we forgive those that trespass against us.' We are offered forgiveness on no other terms. To refuse it is to refuse God's mercy for ourselves. There is no hint of exceptions and God means what he says.

FROM 'ON FORGIVENESS'

IN *FERN-SEED AND ELEPHANTS*

Worlds Beyond

JOY IS THE
SERIOUS BUSINESS
OF HEAVEN.

FROM
LETTERS TO MALCOLM

THE RAZOR'S EDGE

In some sense, as dark to the intellect as it is unendurable to the feelings, we can be both banished from the presence of him who is present everywhere and erased from the knowledge of him who knows all. We can be left utterly and absolutely outside – repelled, exiled, estranged, finally and unspeakably ignored. On the other hand, we can be called in, welcomed, received, acknowledged. We walk every day on the razor edge between these two incredible possibilities. Apparently, then, our lifelong nostalgia, our longing to be reunited with something in the universe from which we now feel cut off, to be on the inside of some door which we have always seen from the outside, is no mere neurotic fancy, but the truest index of our real situation. And to be at last summoned inside would be both glory and honour beyond all our merits and also the healing of that old ache.

FROM *THE WEIGHT OF GLORY*

REALITY ITSELF

'What happens to [the Saved] is best described as the opposite of a mirage. What seemed, when they entered it, to be the vale of misery turns out, when they look back, to have been a well; and where present experience saw only salt deserts, memory truthfully records that the pools were full of water.'

'Then those people are right who say Heaven and Hell are only states of mind?'

'Hush,' said he sternly. 'Do not blaspheme. Hell is a state of mind – ye never said a truer word. And every state of mind, left to itself, every shutting up of the creature within the dungeon of its own mind – is, in the end, Hell. But Heaven is not a state of mind. Heaven is reality itself. All that is fully real is Heavenly. For all that can be shaken will be shaken and only the unshakeable remains.'

FROM *THE GREAT DIVORCE*

THE FINAL CURTAIN

The doctrine of the second coming teaches us that we do not and cannot know when the world drama will end. The curtain may be rung down at any moment: say, before you have finished reading this paragraph... We do not even know whether we are in Act I or Act V. We do not know who are the major and who the minor characters. The Author knows. The audience, if there is an audience (if angels and archangels and all the company of heaven fill the pit and the stalls), may have an inkling. But we, never seeing the play from outside, never meeting any characters except the tiny minority who are 'on' in the same scenes as ourselves, wholly ignorant of the future and very imperfectly informed about the past, cannot tell at what moment the end ought to come. That it will come when it ought, we may be sure; but we waste our time in guessing when that will be. That it has a meaning we may be sure, but we cannot see it. When it is over, we may be told. We are led to expect that the Author will have something to say to each of us on the part that each of us has played. The playing it well is what matters infinitely.

FROM 'THE WORLD'S LAST NIGHT' IN *FERN-SEED AND ELEPHANTS*

THE GREAT DANCE

'He has immeasurable use for each thing that is made, that his love and splendour may flow forth like a strong river which has need of a great water-course and fills alike the deep pools and the little crannies, that are filled equally and remain unequal; and when it has filled them brim full it flows over and makes new channels. We also have need beyond measure of all that he has made. Love me my brothers, for I am infinitely necessary to you and for your delight I was made. Blessed be he!

'All that is made seems planless to the darkened mind, because there are more plans than it looked for. In these seas there are islands where the hairs of the turf are so fine and so closely woven together that unless a man looked long at them he would see neither hairs nor weaving at all, but only the same and the flat. So with the Great Dance. Set your eyes on one movement and it will lead you through all patterns and it will seem to you the master movement. But the seeming will be true. Let no mouth open to gainsay it. There seems no plan because it is all plan: there seems no centre because it is all centre. Blessed be he!'

FROM *VOYAGE TO VENUS*

FAREWELL TO SHADOWLANDS

Then Aslan turned to them and said: 'You do not yet look so happy as I mean you to be.'

Lucy said, 'We're so afraid of being sent away, Aslan. And you have sent us back into our own world so often.'

'No fear of that,' said Aslan. 'Have you not guessed?'

Their hearts leaped and a wild hope rose within them.

'There *was* a real railway accident,' said Aslan softly. 'Your father and mother and all of you are – as you used to call it in the Shadowlands – dead. The term is over: the holidays have begun. The dream is ended: this is the morning.'

And as he spoke he no longer looked to them like a lion; but the things that began to happen after that were so great and beautiful that I cannot write them. And for us this is the end of all the stories, and we can most truly say that they all lived happily ever after. But for them it was only the beginning of the real story.

All their life in this world and all their adventures in Narnia had only been the cover and the title page: now at last they were beginning Chapter One of the Great Story which no one on earth has read: which goes on for ever: in which every chapter is better than the one before.

FROM *THE LAST BATTLE*

TEXT ACKNOWLEDGMENTS

Extracts from *The Problem of Pain, Mere Christianity, The Great Divorce, God In the Dock, Fern-Seed and Elephants, The Weight of Glory, Reflections on the Psalms, Surprised By Joy, The Last Battle* and *The Screwtape Letters* by C.S. Lewis, reproduced by permission of HarperCollins Publishers Ltd (UK).

Extracts from *Screwtape Proposes a Toast, Letters to Malcolm: Chiefly on Prayer, Undeceptions, Poems* and *The Four Loves* by C.S. Lewis, reproduced by permission of HarperCollins Publishers Ltd (UK).

Excerpt from *The Four Loves*, by C.S. Lewis, copyright © 1960 by Helen Joy Lewis and renewed 1988 by Arthur Owen Barfield, reprinted by permission of Harcourt Brace & Company (US).

Excerpt from 'Screwtape Proposes a Toast', in *The World's Last Night and Other Essays* by C.S. Lewis, copyright © 1959 by Helen Joy Lewis and renewed 1987 by Arthur Owen Barfield, reprinted by permission of Harcourt Brace & Company (US).

'Prayer' from *Poems* by C.S. Lewis, copyright © 1964 by The Executors of the Estate of C.S. Lewis and renewed 1992 by C.S. Lewis Pte. Ltd, reprinted by permission of Harcourt Brace & Company (US).

Excerpt from *Letters to Malcolm: Chiefly on Prayer* by C.S. Lewis, copyright © 1964, 1963 by C.S. Lewis Pte. Ltd and renewed 1992, 1991 by Arthur Owen Barfield, reprinted by permission of Harcourt Brace & Company (US).

Extract from *God In the Dock* copyright © 1970 by C.S. Lewis Pty Ltd, reproduced by permission of Curtis Brown, London.

Extract from *Perelandra* by C.S. Lewis – The Bodley Head, published by Random House UK Ltd. Reproduced by permission of Random House UK Ltd.